KS2 Success

Age 10-11

Challenging Maths

Revision & Practice

Paul Broadbent and Gillian Rich

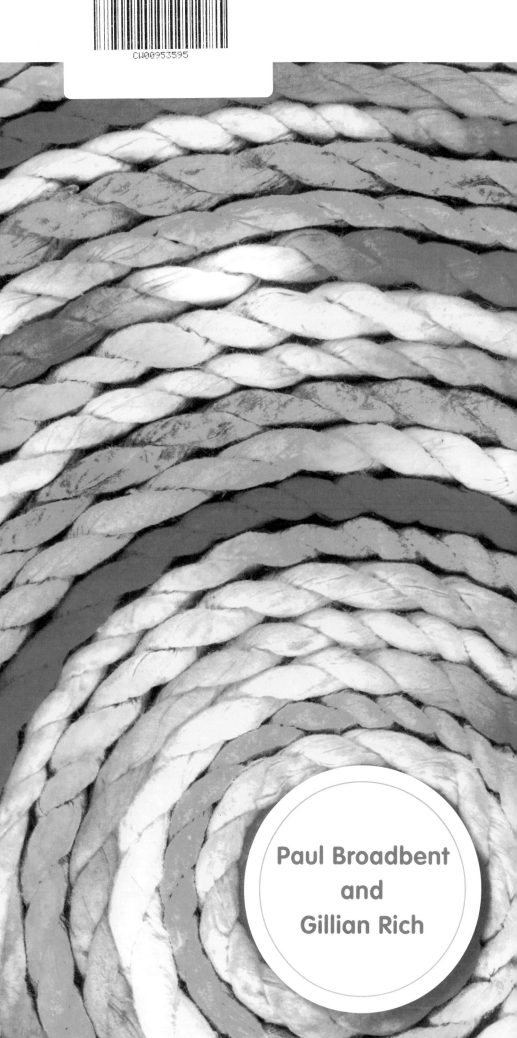

Contents

Statistics

Glossary

Answers

Types of numbers

Ordering numbers

A positive number (+) is a number greater than zero. For example, +4.
A negative number (–) is a number less than zero. For example, –4.

The + sign is not necessary. If there is no sign, assume that the number is positive.

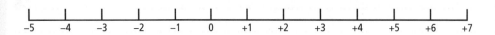

Use the number line for number facts:

–4 < +1   –4 is less than +1   –2 > –5   –2 is greater than –5   –2 < +2   –2 is less than +2

Adding and subtracting positive and negative numbers

Adding

When you add a positive number to another positive number, the answer is a number further to the right on a number line (see the number line above).

$3 + (+4) = 7$

Start at +3 and move 4 to the right.

When you add a negative number to a positive number, the answer is a number further to the left on a number line.

$3 + (–4) = –1$

Start at +3 and move 4 to the left.

Subtracting

Subtracting is the reverse of adding.

When you subtract a positive number from another positive number, the answer is a number further to the left on a number line.

$3 – (+4) = –1$

Start at +3 and move 4 to the left.

When you subtract a negative number from a positive number, the answer is a number further to the right on a number line.

$3 – (–4) = 7$

Start at +3 and move 4 to the right.

Using positive and negative numbers

Positive and negative numbers are commonly used to discuss temperature.

If the temperature is –5°C and it rises 6 degrees, what will the temperature be?

$–5°C + 6°C = +1°C$

Keywords	positive number negative number number line

Ordering numbers

1 Insert < or >.

   a   5 ☐ 6   b   3 ☐ 2   c   75 ☐ 53

   d   11 ☐ 22   e   1.75 ☐ 5.32

2 Put each list of numbers in order, starting with the smallest first.

   a   2, –7, 5, –6, 8, –1   _____

   b   –12, 11, 4, –17, 12, –11   _____

   c   –7, 8, 4, 6, –9, –5   _____

   d   –4, 9, –3, 3, –5, 6   _____

   e   8, –2, 1, –3, –8, 4   _____   `10`

Adding and subtracting positive and negative numbers

1 Work out the answers to the problems below.

   a   (–3) + (–6) = _____   b   (–13) – (+4) = _____

   c   (–29) – (–29) = _____   d   (+14) + (–5) = _____

   e   (+32) – (+7) = _____   `5`

Using positive and negative numbers

1 What is the temperature after (i) a drop of 5 degrees (ii) a rise of 7 degrees?

   a   16°C   i _____   ii _____

   b   5°C   i _____   ii _____

   c   –12°C   i _____   ii _____

   d   –6°C   i _____   ii _____

   e   0°C   i _____   ii _____

2 In this number square, the sum of each row, column and diagonal is the same. Find the missing numbers.

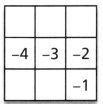

    `10`

TOTAL MARKS ☐ 25   **5**

Fractions, decimals, percentages

Equivalent values

Percentages are **fractions** out of 100 – that is what *per cent* means: out of 100. % is the percentage sign.

In a box of 100 tiles, 25 are red. 25% of the tiles are red, which is $\frac{1}{4}$ of the tiles. Another box of 20 tiles has 5 red tiles. This also means 25% of the tiles are red.

To change fractions to percentages, make them out of 100. This means you need to find an **equivalent** fraction with the **denominator** 100.

$\frac{3}{5}$ is equivalent to $\frac{60}{100}$, so $\frac{3}{5}$ = 60%

If you find it easier, write the fraction as a decimal and then multiply by 100. $\frac{3}{4}$ is 0.75, which is the same as 75%.

Top tip!

To change a percentage to a fraction, write the percentage as a fraction out of 100 and then reduce it to its lowest terms.

40% is $\frac{40}{100}$, which is the same as $\frac{2}{5}$ 5% is $\frac{5}{100}$, which is the same as $\frac{1}{20}$

When you change **decimals** to tenths or hundredths, cancel the fraction to its lowest terms.

$0.23 = \frac{23}{100}$ $0.24 = \frac{24}{100} = \frac{6}{25}$

Change fractions to decimals by dividing the **numerator** by the denominator.

$\frac{1}{2} = 0.5$ $\frac{60}{100} = 0.6$

It is a good idea to memorise these. Cover up different boxes in the table and work out the covered amounts.

Decimal	0.1	0.2	0.3	0.4	0.5	0.6	0.7	0.8	0.9	0.25	0.75
Fraction	$\frac{1}{10}$	$\frac{1}{5}$	$\frac{3}{10}$	$\frac{2}{5}$	$\frac{1}{2}$	$\frac{3}{5}$	$\frac{7}{10}$	$\frac{4}{5}$	$\frac{9}{10}$	$\frac{1}{4}$	$\frac{3}{4}$
Percentage	10%	20%	30%	40%	50%	60%	70%	80%	90%	25%	75%

Keywords	percentage fraction equivalent denominator
	decimal numerator

REVISE

NUMBER AND ALGEBRA

Equivalent values

1 Change these decimals to fractions.

a 0.43 _____

b 0.57 _____

c 0.24 _____

d 2.65 _____

2 Change these fractions to decimals.

a $\frac{3}{4}$ _____

b $\frac{2}{5}$ _____

c $\frac{5}{8}$ _____

d $4\frac{1}{3}$ _____

3 Change these percentages to fractions and decimals.

a 25%   Fraction: _____   Decimal: _____

b 40%   Fraction: _____   Decimal: _____

c 5%   Fraction: _____   Decimal: _____

d 88%   Fraction: _____   Decimal: _____

If you are asked to convert a percentage to a decimal, remember that it will always be less than 1.

Top tip!

4 Change these fractions and decimals to percentages.

a $\frac{3}{5}$ _____

b $\frac{4}{25}$ _____

c $\frac{17}{20}$ _____

d $\frac{43}{50}$ _____

e 0.67 _____

f 0.59 _____

g 0.125 _____

h 0.375 _____

5 Write <, > or = to make each statement true.

a 35% [ ] 0.35

b 0.85 [ ] 58%

c 6% [ ] 0.6

d 0.9 [ ] 90%

e 2% [ ] 0.02

f $\frac{4}{5}$ [ ] 0.8

30

Ratio

Ratio and proportion

Ratio is used to compare one amount with another. What is the ratio of green to orange tiles in the pattern below?

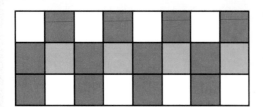

There are 4 green tiles and 12 orange tiles. For every 1 green tile, there are 3 orange tiles. The ratio of green to orange is 1 to 3, or 1:3.

This ratio stays the same for different amounts:

Green	1	2	3	4	5	6
Orange	3	6	9	12	15	18

Using the ratio of 1:3, 24 of these green and orange tiles would be divided into 6 green tiles and 18 orange tiles.

How many green tiles are needed if 60 tiles are used in the pattern shown above?

The proportion of tiles that are green is 1 in every 6, or $\frac{1}{6}$.

This means that in a set of 60 tiles, 10 would be green.

Ratios are a bit like fractions – they can both be simplified by finding the highest common factors. For example, in a class of 16 boys and 12 girls, the ratio of boys to girls is 16:12. This can be simplified by dividing by 4 to give a ratio of 4:3.

Top tip!

Direct proportion

Two quantities are in direct proportion when they increase or decrease in the same ratio. For example, if 3 pens cost 90p, what is the cost of 15 pens?

This is five times the number of pens, so it is five times the price. 90p × 5 = £4.50

Scale drawings and maps are examples of ways we use direct proportion.

This car is drawn at a scale of 50:1.
The drawing is 4.6cm long.
How long is the actual car?

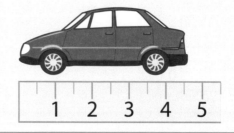

1 2 3 4 5

4.6cm × 50 = 230cm = 2.3m

Keywords	ratio proportion direct proportion

Ratio and proportion

1 Simplify these ratios.

a   4:6 _____   b   25:100 _____

c   6:18:24 _____   d   28:35:70 _____

2 Divide these amounts in the given ratios.

a   £144 in the ratio 3:5 _____

b   750g in the ratio 3:7 _____

c   480ml in the ratio 7:9 _____

d   2700km in the ratio 4:5 _____

8

Direct proportion

Work out the following.

1 4 cans of beans cost £1.20. How much will:

a   8 cost? _____

b   12 cost? _____

2 If £1 is worth $1.52, how many dollars will Jacob get for £100?

_____

3 A fruit crumble for 4 people uses 250g flour, 128g sugar, 128g margarine and 450g apples. What are the amounts needed for:

a   8 people?

Flour: _____ [ ]   Sugar: _____ [ ]

Margarine: _____ [ ]   Apples: _____ [ ]

b   6 people?

Flour: _____ [ ]   Sugar: _____ [ ]

Margarine: _____ [ ]   Apples: _____ [ ]

11

Multiples, factors and primes

Multiples

A multiple is a number made by multiplying together two other numbers.

Look at these multiples of 6 and 8.

Multiples of 6 ➜ 6, 12, 18, **24**, 30, 36 ...

Multiples of 8 ➜ 8, 16, **24**, 32, 40, 48 ...

The lowest common multiple (LCM) of 6 and 8 is 24.

Factors

Factors are numbers that will divide exactly into other numbers. It is useful to put factors of numbers into pairs:

Factors of 30 ➜ (1 and 30), (2 and 15), (3 and 10), (5 and 6) = 8 factors

Factors of 45 ➜ (1 and 45), (3 and 15), (5 and 9) = 6 factors

If you look at the factors of 30 and 45, there are some factors that are the same for both numbers. The numbers 1, 3, 5 and 15 are common factors of 30 and 45.

15 is the largest number which is a common factor of 30 and 45, which means that the highest common factor (HCF) of 30 and 45 is 15.

Top tip! *Highest common factors are used to simplify equivalent fractions. For example, $\frac{32}{56}$ can be simplified to $\frac{4}{7}$ by dividing by the HCF of 32 and 56, which is 8.*

Primes

A prime number only has two factors: 1 and itself. For example, 23 is a prime number as it can only be divided by 1 and 23. The number 1 is not a prime number as it only has one factor.

The prime factors of a number are all those factors of the number which are prime numbers.

All the factors of 28 are 1, 2, 4, 7, 14 and 28. The prime factors of 28 are 2 and 7.

Keywords	multiple lowest common multiple factor
	highest common factor prime number prime factor

Multiples

Find the first five multiples of the following numbers.

1 4 _____

2 5 _____

3 7 _____

4 10 _____

5 12 _____

6 20 _____

6

Factors

1 List the factors of the following numbers.

a   15 _____

b   16 _____

c   20 _____

d   24 _____

e   30 _____

f   45 _____

2 Find the LCM and the HCF of the following numbers.

a   12 and 20   LCM: _____   HCF: _____

b   8 and 14   LCM: _____   HCF: _____

c   10 and 35   LCM: _____   HCF: _____

d   15 and 18   LCM: _____   HCF: _____

e   30 and 45   LCM: _____   HCF: _____

f   9 and 36   LCM: _____   HCF: _____

18

Primes

List the primes between the following numbers.

1 20 and 30 _____

2 32 and 42 _____

3 70 and 80 _____

4 90 and 100 _____

4

TOTAL MARKS 28

Algebra

Letters in algebra

In algebra, letters or symbols are used to represent unknown values.

$3a$ means $3 \times a$ or 3 lots of a. This is the same as $a + a + a$.
a is the unknown value and 3 is the **coefficient**.

An **expression** is a statement containing numbers and letters, for example $3c + 4d$. $3c$ and $4d$ are called terms.

If the coefficient = 1, it does not need to be written down.

Top tip!

An **equation** connects two expressions. It must have an equals sign, for example $n + 5 = 9$. n is the unknown value. An equation can be solved to find the unknown value. If $n + 5 = 9$, then subtract 5 from both sides giving $n = 4$.

The following examples show you how to use letters in algebra.

$n + 6$	Add 6 to a number
$n - 3$	Subtract 3 from a number
$5n + 2$	Multiply a number by 5 and then add 2

$5n$ is not the same as $5 + n$

$n \div 3$ or $\frac{n}{3}$	Divide a number by 3
$8(n + 4)$	Add 4 to a number and multiply the answer by 8

$8(n + 4)$ is not the same as $8n + 4$

$n \times n$ or n^2	Multiply a number by itself

n^2 is not the same as $2n$

Working with letters

When adding or subtracting in algebra, remember these rules:
- $a + a + a + a = 4a$
- $a + b$ is the same as $b + a$
- $a + a + b + b = 2a + 2b$
- $a - b$ is **not** the same as $b - a$

When multiplying in algebra, remember these rules:
- $5 \times a = 5a$
- $2 \times (a + b) = 2(a + b)$
- $3 \times a - a \times b = 3a - ab$
- $a \times (b \times c) = (a \times b) \times c$ or $a(bc) = (ab)c = abc$

When dividing in algebra, remember these rules:
- $5 \div a = \frac{5}{a}$
- $(3 \div a) - (2 \div b) = \frac{3}{a} - \frac{2}{b}$
- $2 \div (a + b) = \frac{2}{(a + b)}$

Keywords	coefficient expression equation

Letters in algebra

1 Rewrite these statements as expressions, using c as the unknown number.

a Add 11 to a number   _____

b Subtract a number from 10   _____

c 6 minus a number   _____

d A number multiplied by 4 and then 3 is added   _____

e 2 multiplies a number and 5 is subtracted   _____

f 15 divided by a number   _____

g A number plus 3 then multiplied by 2   _____

2 Write these as expressions.

a 2 more than a _____   b 4 less than b _____

c $3c$ more than $2n$ _____   d $5d$ less than m _____

11

Working with letters

1 Simplify the following additions and subtractions.

a $p + p + p + p + p + p + p + p$ _____

b $q + q + q + q + q + q + q + r + r + r + r + r$ _____

c $s + s + s + s - t + t$ _____

d $x + x + x + x + x - y + y + y$ _____

2 Simplify the following.

a $3 \times 4 \times a$ _____   b $2 \times m - 5 \times n + m \times n$ _____

c $2 \div c$ _____   d $(a \times b + b \times c) \div (c \times d)$ _____

3 Which number does the letter represent in each of the following equations?

a $3a = 12$ _____   b $\dfrac{b}{5} = 4$ _____

c $c + 7 = 18$ _____   d $2(d + 3) = 16$ _____

12

TOTAL MARKS 23

Expressions

Forming an expression

An **expression** can be formed by translating information into letters and numbers.

For example, think of a number. First add 4, and then double the result.
This can be written as an expression using y as the unknown number: $2(y + 4)$.

Write expressions for the area and perimeter of this rectangle.

The area of the rectangle is its length multiplied by its width: $l \times w = lw$

The perimeter of the rectangle is the sum of its four sides: $l + w + l + w = 2l + 2w$

Simplifying expressions

Simplifying expressions involves collecting similar terms together, as in the perimeter example above. This is called **collecting like terms**.

$a + a + a - a + b - b - b = 2a - b$

> Collect the same letter terms.

$2a - 3b + 3b + 1 = 2a + 1$

> Integers without a letter count as a different term.

$3x^2 + xy - x^2 + y^2 = 2x^2 + xy + y^2$

> Terms with the same letter and index can be collected; terms with xy cannot be combined with x terms or y terms.

When simplifying expressions involving brackets make sure you multiply out the brackets first. Multiply each term in the bracket by the number outside the bracket. Then collect like terms as before. For example:

$2(c + 3d) + 3(2c - d) = 2c + 6d + 6c - 3d = 8c + 3d$

$4n(1 + n) + n(1 - n) = 4n + 4n^2 + n - n^2 = 5n + 3n^2$

 Top tip!

Remember to check the sign in front of the term.

Substituting in expressions

The value of an expression can be found by substituting given values into the expression.

When $p = 3$, $q = 5$, $r = 2$ the value of these expressions can be worked out.
$p + q + r = 3 + 5 + 2 = 10$
$pqr = p \times q \times r = 3 \times 5 \times 2 = 30$
$p(q + r) = p \times (q + r) = 3 \times (5 + 2) = 3 \times 7 = 21$

Keywords		expression simplify

Forming an expression

① In a test Miriam got *m* marks. Write down expressions for these statements.

  a   Sam got 5 marks more than Miriam. _____

  b   Jake got twice as many marks as Miriam and Sam got together.

  _____

② a   Naomi plants bulbs in the garden. She plants daffodils (*d*), tulips (*t*) and crocuses (*c*). Write down expressions for the number of bulbs in the following:

   i a row of 5 daffodils and 12 crocuses. _____

   ii 3 rows of 10 tulips. _____

   iii 4 tubs each having 3 tulips and 5 crocuses. _____

  b   Naomi plants a total of 50 daffodils, 24 tulips and 60 crocuses. Slugs eat $\frac{1}{10}$ of the daffodils, $\frac{1}{8}$ of the tulips and $\frac{1}{4}$ of the crocuses. How many bulbs are left? _____

  _____

③ A school has two types of minibus. 12 are painted red and hold r passengers. 8 are painted white and hold w passengers.

  Write an expression for the total number of passengers the minibuses can transport if they are all used and are all full.

  _____

 7

Simplifying expressions

① Collect the like terms in these expressions.

  a $3a + 4 + 2b - a - 3$ _____

  b $4(8 + c) + 2(c - 5)$ _____

  c $d^2 - 5d - 2d + 3d^2$ _____

  d $2f + \frac{6(f + 3)}{3}$ _____

4

Substituting in expressions

① Find the value of the following expressions when *x* = 2, *y* = 1, *z* = 3.

  a   *xyz* _____

  b $xy + yz + zx$ _____

  c $\frac{2xyz}{3}$ _____

  d $4(x^2y + y^2z + z^2x)$ _____

 4

TOTAL MARKS 15

Sequences

Number sequences

A number sequence is a set of numbers that follow a given rule or pattern. Each number in the sequence is called a term. Terms next to each other are called consecutive terms. Consecutive terms are separated by commas, for example, 3, 6, 9, 12, ...

Here are some examples of number patterns:

Counting numbers: 1, 2, 3, 4, 5, 6, ...

Even numbers: 2, 4, 6, 8, 10, 12, ...

Odd numbers: 1, 3, 5, 7, 9, 11, ...

Square numbers: 1, 4, 9, 16, 25, 36, ...

Cube numbers: 1, 8, 27, 64, 125, ...

Triangular numbers: 1, 3, 6, 10, 15, ...

Using shape patterns

Some sequences can be illustrated by using shapes.

Odd numbers: 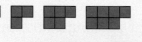   Even numbers:

Square numbers:    Triangular numbers: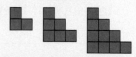

Generating terms of a sequence

If you are given the first term and the 'term-to-term' rule, a sequence can be generated.

First term 2, term-to-term rule 'add 4'	2, 6, 10, 14, ... +4 +4 +4	Difference is +4
First term 100, term-to-term rule 'subtract 5'	100, 95, 90, 85, ... −5 −5 −5	Difference is −5
First term 3, term-to-term rule 'double'	3, 6, 12, 24, 48, ... ×2 ×2 ×2 ×2	Multiply by 2
First term 5, term-to-term rule '5 times'	5, 25, 125, 625, ... ×5 ×5 ×5 ×5	Multiply by 5

Top tip!

Look at the difference between numbers in a sequence to help you work out the rule.

| Keywords | sequence   term   triangular number |

Number sequences

Write down the next three terms in these sequences.

1 Even numbers after 24. _____

2 Multiples of 3 after 63. _____

3 Square numbers after 49. _____

4 Cube numbers after 64. _____

[4]

Using shape patterns

Draw the next two patterns in these sequence patterns.

1

2

[2]

Generating terms of a sequence

Find the next two terms in these sequences.

1 First term 5, term-to-term rule 'add 3'.

5, 8, 11, 14, _____, _____, ...

2 First term 100, term-to-term rule 'subtract 4'.

100, 96, 92, 88, _____, _____, ...

3 First term 1000, term-to-term rule 'halve'.

1000, 500, 250, 125, _____, _____, ...

4 First term 5, term-to-term rule '×3'.

5, 15, 45, 135, _____, _____, ...

[4]

TOTAL MARKS [10]

*n*th term

Further generating terms of a sequence

The **nth term** is a general rule for finding any term in a sequence. *n* stands for the position of the term.

*n*th term = *n* + 2; 10th term = 10 + 2 = 12   Substitute *n* = 10 in *n*th term.

*n*th term = 3*n*; 15th term = 3 × 15 = 45   Substitute *n* = 15 in *n*th term.

*n*th term = 4*n* − 1; 12th term = 4 × 12 − 1 = 47   Substitute *n* = 12 in *n*th term.

*n*th term = 2*n*^{2}; 10th term = 2 × 10 × 10 = 200   Substitute *n* = 10 in *n*th term.

*n*th term = *n*^{3} + 1; 20th term = 20 × 20 × 20 + 1 = 8001   Substitute *n* = 20 in *n*th term.

*n*th term = $\frac{n^2}{2}$; 50th term = $\frac{50 \times 50}{2}$ = 1250   Substitute *n* = 50 in *n*th term.

Finding the *n*th term

The *n*th term of a sequence can be found by looking at the number pattern.

The terms in the number pattern 2, 4, 6, 8, 10, … can be found by adding 2 each time.

1st term = 2 (or 2 × 1)

2nd term = 2 + 2 = 4 (or 2 × 2)

3rd term = 2 + 2 + 2 = 6 (or 2 × 3)

*n*th term = 2 × *n* = 2*n*

The position of the term equals the number of '2's.

The terms in the number pattern 7, 12, 17, 22, 27, … can be found by adding 5 each time.

1st term = 7

2nd term = 7 + 5 = 12

3rd term = 7 + 5 + 5 = 17

4th term = 7 + 5 + 5 + 5 = 22

5th term = 7 + 5 + 5 + 5 + 5 = 27

*n*th term = 7 + 5(*n* − 1) = 7 + 5*n* − 5 = 5*n* + 2

The number of '5's added each time is one less than the position of the term.

Keywords	*n*th term

Further generating terms of a sequence

1 Find the 20th term in these sequences.

   a nth term = $n - 2$ _____

   b nth term = $5n$ _____

   c nth term = $3n + 1$ _____

   d nth term = $4n^2$ _____

   e nth term = $2n - 1$ _____

2 Find the following.

   a nth term = $4n^2$
      7th term = _____

   b nth term = $2n + 6$
      10th term = _____

   c nth term = $4n + 3$
      12th term = _____

   d nth term = $3n + 10$
      30th term = _____

   e nth term = $5n - 2$
      50th term = _____

10

Finding the nth term

1 Find the nth term for each of the following sequences.

   a   1, 4, 7, 10, 13, … _____

   b   2, 6, 10, 14, 18, … _____

   c   3, 7, 11, 15, 19, … _____

   d   26, 24, 22, 20, 18, … _____

   e   3, 5, 7, 9, 11, … _____

   f   4, 7, 10, 13, 16, … _____

   g   2, 5, 10, 17, 26, … _____

   h   2, 1, 0, –1, –2, … _____

8

TOTAL MARKS   18

Equations

Forming equations

When forming an equation you need to understand what the letter in the equation represents.

4 is added to a number (y) and then the result is doubled. The answer is 14. This can be written as an equation and used to find the unknown number y.

$2(y + 4) = 14$

If $2 \times (y + 4) = 14$, then $(y + 4) = \dfrac{14}{2} = 7$ ←————— Use the opposite operation.

If $y + 4 = 7$, then y must be 3.

A pile of books is 20cm high. Each book is 2cm thick. This can be written as an equation and used to find the number of books (b) in the pile.

$2b = 20$

If $2 \times b = 20$, then $b = \dfrac{20}{2} = 10$

The number of books in the pile is 10.

Always give the answer in the terms of the question.

Top tip!

Solving equations

Equations use symbols or letters instead of numbers in a calculation, for example ■ + 2 = 15, 4▲ − 5 = 19, $3y + 9 = 24$, etc.

You need to work out what the symbol or letter stands for, so use the numbers given to help you.

Equations need to stay balanced. If you add or take away a number from one side, do the same to the other side, so the equation stays the same. It's a good way of working out the letter.

Top tip!

Try working out, step-by-step, $3y + 9 = 24$

1   You want y on one side of the equation and the numbers on the other. Subtract 9 from both sides. If it were −9, you would add 9 to both sides. $3y = 24 − 9$ so $3y = 15$

2   Say the equation as a sentence: 3 times something makes 15. So $y = 5$

3   Test it with the original equation: $(3 \times 5) + 9 = 24$, so y *is* equal to 5

Forming equations

Form an equation to help you answer each question.

1 A number is multiplied by 8 and 3 is added. The answer is 59.

What is the number? _____

2 The three angles of a triangle total 180°. A triangle has three angles: t, $t + 15$ and $t + 30$. What are the three angles in the triangle?

Equation: _____

The three angles: _____

3 Gary has a bag of k marbles.

a   He plays a game and wins five more marbles, which he puts in the bag.

Write an equation to say how many marbles he has got now. _____

b   He plays a second game and wins again. He doubles the number of marbles in the bag.

Write an equation for how many marbles are now in the bag.

_____

c   When he gets home, he counts the marbles in the bag. There are 42 marbles.

Form an equation from the information given in **a** and **b** and solve it to find how many marbles were in the bag at the beginning.

_____

_____

[5]

Solving equations

Solve these equations.

1 $2a = 40$ _____

2 $15b = 60$ _____

3 $b + 13 = 25$ _____

4 $c - 4 = 17$ _____

5 $c - 12 = 38$ _____

6 $2d + 9 = 31$ _____

7 $5d + 16 = 56$ _____

8 $\frac{e}{5} = 7$ _____

[8]

TOTAL MARKS [13]   21

More equations

Solving more equations

In the equation below, the brackets can be multiplied out and then the equation can be solved.

$2(f + 5) = 15$

$2f + 10 = 15$ — Multiply out brackets

$2f = 15 - 10 = 5$ — 10 is added to 2f, so subtract 10 from 15 to find 2f

$f = \dfrac{5}{2}$ — f is multiplied by 2, so divide 5 by 2 to find f

$f = 2.5$

When the letter is on the right-hand side of the equals sign, it is solved in the same way as an equation with the letter on the left-hand side of the equals sign.

$8 = 3g - 4$

$8 + 4 = 3g$

$12 = 3g$

$g = \dfrac{12}{3} = 4$

Trial and improvement

If an equation cannot be solved easily, an approximate solution can be found using the **trial and improvement** method.

Use the trial and improvement method to find a positive solution of $x^3 + x = 20$. Give your answer to 1 decimal place.
First substitute values in the left-hand side of the equation. Check the answer against the right-hand side of the equation.

x	$x^3 + x$	Comment
2	8 + 2 = 10	Too small
3	27 + 3 = 30	Too large
2.5	15.63 + 2.5 = 18.13	Too small
2.6	17.58 + 2.6 = 20.18	Too large
2.59	17.37 + 2.59 = 19.96	Too small

x must be between 2 and 3

x must be between 2.5 and 2.6

$x = 2.59$ is just too small and $x = 2.6$ is just too large. Both these values give an approximate solution of $x = 2.6$ to 1 decimal place.

Keywords

trial and improvement

Solving more equations

1 a $3(f + 6) = 18$ _____ b $6(3 + f) = 42$ _____

2 a $2(3 + a) = 28$ _____ b $6(b - 2) = 54$ _____

3 a $9 = 2g - 5$ _____ b $32 = 11 + 3g$ _____

4 a $24 = 3(a - 1)$ _____ b $16 = 4(b + 2)$ _____

8

Trial and improvement

Find the approximate positive solutions to these equations using the trial and improvement method. Give your answers to 1 decimal place.

1 $x^2 + 3x = 6$

x	$x^2 + 3x$	Comment

2 $x^3 - 8x = 110$

x	$x^3 - 8x$	Comment

4

TOTAL MARKS 12 23

Formulae

Using a formula

A **formula** is used to find an unknown quantity, when the other quantities are given.

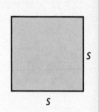

The formula for finding the **perimeter** of this square is $P = 4s$ where P = the perimeter and s = the side of the square. The four sides of a square are equal.

If the value for either P or s is given, the other value can be found.

Substituting in a formula

Values can be substituted into a formula to find a missing quantity. Look at this rectangle:

l = the length w = the width A = the area

P = the perimeter $A = lw$ $P = 2(l + w)$

Find the area and perimeter when l = 8cm and w = 6cm.

Area = $A = l \times w = 8 \times 6 = 48\text{cm}^2$

Substitute the given values into the formula before calculating, otherwise mistakes can be made.

Top tip!

$$\begin{aligned} \text{Perimeter} = P &= 2(l + w) \\ &= 2(8 + 6) \\ &= 2 \times 14 \\ &= 28\text{cm} \end{aligned}$$

Deriving a formula

A statement can be converted into a formula, using appropriate letters. Remember to define each letter.

- A week has 7 days: $W = 7d$ where W = a week and d = a day.

- A year (Y) has a months of 31 days each, b months of 30 days each and c months of 28 days. So this is a formula for the number of days in a year when it is not a leap year:

$Y = 31a + 30b + 28c$

Keywords

formula   perimeter   area

Using a formula

Use the formula $A = lw$ for questions 1–3.

1 Find the area of these rectangles.

    a l = 5cm, w = 3cm   _____
    b l = 6cm, w = 2.5cm   _____

2 Find the length of these rectangles.

    a A = 24cm^2, w = 3cm   _____
    b A = 40cm^2, w = 5cm   _____

3 Find the perimeter of these rectangles.

    a A = 45cm^2, l = 15cm   _____
    b A = 40cm^2, w = 5cm   _____

4 Use the formula $P = 4s$ to find the perimeter of the square in **a** and the side of the square in **b**.

    a s = 6cm P = _____
    b P = 100mm s = _____

    8

Substituting in a formula

Find the missing values in the following formulae.

1 $y = mx + c$

    a x = 3, m = 2, c = 1   _____
    b y = 8, m = 3, x = 0   _____

2 $A = kr^2$

    a k = 2, r = 3   _____
    b A = 100, k = 4   _____

3 $s = \dfrac{D}{t}$

    a D = 150, t = 3   _____
    b s = 30, t = 1.5   _____

  6

Deriving a formula

Write down a formula for each of these statements.

1 The cost (C) of m pencils each costing 27 pence.   _____

2 The number of centimetres (c) in a length of wood measuring n metres.   _____

3 The change (C) received from £10 after buying y stamps at 30p each.   _____

4 The pence (p) in L pounds.   _____

  4

TOTAL MARKS   18   **25**

Functions

Functions and mappings

This **function machine** shows the **mapping** of *x* onto *y*.

| *x* | → | Multiply by 3 | → | Add 2 | → | *y* |

The output *y* can be found for every input of *x*. This table gives some of the results.

Input (*x*)	1	2	3	4	5	6
Output (*y*)	5	8	11	14	17	20

This function can also be given by $x \rightarrow 3x + 2$ or $f(x) = 3x + 2$

The function is missing here: 1, 2, 4, 7 → [   ] → 4, 8, 16, 28

Each input number appears to be multiplied by 4 to get each output number.

So, the function can be given by $x \rightarrow 4x$ or $f(x) = 4x$

Coordinates

Coordinates are pairs of points which are plotted on a grid. They can be joined to form shapes or lines. Coordinates are written in brackets (*x*, *y*). The *x*-coordinate is given first. There is a comma between the two values.

Always plot the *x*-coordinate on the horizontal **axis** and the *y*-coordinate on the vertical axis and label the axes *x* and *y*. Mark the axes in regular steps.

Results from function machine tables can be plotted using coordinates to illustrate the function.

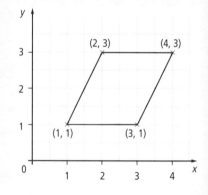

Given a function, a table can be completed, for example, $f(x) = x + 1$ or $y = x + 1$

x	−2	−1	0	1	2
y	−1	0	1	2	3

The point (0, 0) is called the origin.

Top tip!

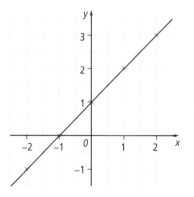

Keywords   function machine   mapping   coordinates   axis   origin

Functions and mappings

1 This function machine shows the mapping of *x* onto *y*.

$$x \;\rightarrow\; \boxed{\text{Add 3}} \;\rightarrow\; \boxed{\text{Multiply by 4}} \;\rightarrow\; y$$

a Complete this table to show the output from this machine.

Input (*x*)	1	2	3	4	5	6
Output (*y*)						

b Write down this function. _____

2 What is the missing function? 1, 6, 3, 7 → ☐ → 3, 18, 9, 21

3

Coordinates

1 Complete these tables.

a $f(x) = x - 1$

x	−2	−1	0	1	2
y					

b $f(x) = x + 2$

x	−2	−1	0	1	2
y					

c Plot the coordinates for tables **1 a** and **b** above.
Join the coordinates for each line.

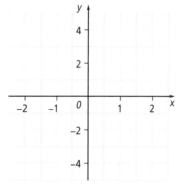

2 Plot these points and join them
together in the order they are given.
What shapes do they make?

a (0, 0), (4, 2),
(3, 4), (−1, 2) _____

b (0, 0), (4, 0), (2, 4) _____

c (−2, −1), (2, −1),
(2, 3), (−2, 3) _____

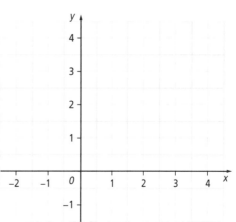

7

TOTAL MARKS ☐ 10

Calculations

Operations of number

In addition and subtraction always make sure the digits are lined up in the correct column for their place value.

$$
\begin{array}{r}
14.367 \\
+\ 9.658 \\
\hline
24.025 \\
\hline
{\scriptstyle 1\quad 11}
\end{array}
$$

$$
\begin{array}{r}
{\scriptstyle 1\ 9\ 1} \\
2.056 \\
-\ 0.164 \\
\hline
1.892 \\
\hline
\end{array}
$$

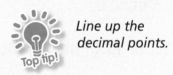

Line up the decimal points.

When multiplying and dividing, always estimate an answer first.

Find the cost of 124 pens at 43p each.
(Estimate ➜ $120 \times 40 = 4800$p or £48)

$$
\begin{array}{r}
124 \\
\times\ \ 43 \\
\hline
372 \ (124 \times 3) \\
4960 \ (124 \times 40) \\
\hline
5332\text{p} = £53.32
\end{array}
$$

105 people are going on a trip using 14-seater minibuses. How many buses should they order?
(Estimate ➜ $100 \div 10 = 10$)

$$
\begin{array}{r}
7 \\
14\overline{)105} \\
-\ 98 \ (14 \times 7) \\
\hline
7
\end{array}
$$

8 buses are needed for the total number of people.

Order of operations

Calculations should be carried out using the following order of operations. Use BIDMAS to help you remember the order:

Brackets: work out any brackets first

Indices or powers: work out squares, cubes or their roots

Division

Multiplication

Addition

Subtraction

$$(4 + 9) \times 2^2 + 21 \div (8 - 5) - 6 = 13 \times 2^2 + 21 \div 3 - 6 \quad \longleftarrow \text{Work out the brackets first.}$$

$$= 13 \times 4 + 21 \div 3 - 6 \quad \longleftarrow \text{Work out the indices next.}$$

$$= 52 + 7 - 6 = 53 \quad \longleftarrow \times \text{ and } \div \text{ then } + \text{ and } -$$

Keywords

digit   place value   estimate
order of operations   BIDMAS

Operations of number

1 Add or subtract the following. Use paper to show your working.

    a   354.7 + 0.09 + 37.842 _____   b 43.25 + 9.006 + 732.9 _____

    c   627.19 – 18.935 _____   d 127.03 – 9.643 _____

2 Multiply or divide the following. Use paper to show your working.

    a 251×17 _____

    b $2484 \div 18$ _____

3 Multiply or divide the following. Use paper to show your working.

    a   One ribbon measures 17.6cm. What is the total length of 18 of these ribbons?

       _____

    b   7245 packets of biscuits are packed in 15 boxes. How many packets are in each box?

       _____

    c   A box of 36 pens costs £19.44. How much does each pen cost?

       _____

9

Order of operations

Calculate the following. Use a separate sheet of paper to show all your working.

1 $(180 \div 6) - 5^2$ _____

2 $(7 \times 3) + (6 \times 4)$ _____

3 $(3 + 5)^2 + (4 - 3)^3$ _____

4 $(750 \div 3) + 2$ _____

4

TOTAL MARKS 13

Calculations with fractions

Fractions of quantities

Finding fractions of quantities is very similar to dividing amounts.

What is $\frac{1}{3}$ of 21?

This has 1 as a numerator, so simply divide by the denominator.

$\frac{1}{3}$ of 21 is $21 \div 3 = 7$

What is $\frac{2}{3}$ of 21?

Now the numerator is 2, so it is double 7. $\frac{2}{3}$ of 21 = 14

Top tip! If the numerator is more than 1, divide by the denominator and then multiply by the numerator.

It is possible to find one quantity as a fraction of another quantity.

What fraction is 5 minutes of 1 hour?

1 hour = 60 minutes   5 minutes = $\frac{5}{60}$ = $\frac{1}{12}$ of 1 hour

Adding and subtracting fractions

If fractions have the same denominator, just add or subtract the numerators:

$$\frac{2}{5} + \frac{1}{5} = \frac{3}{5} \qquad \frac{5}{7} - \frac{3}{7} = \frac{2}{7} \qquad \frac{4}{6} - \frac{1}{6} = \frac{3}{6} = \frac{1}{2} \qquad \frac{5}{8} + \frac{7}{8} = \frac{12}{8} = 1\frac{1}{2}$$

If fractions have different denominators, find their lowest common multiple (LCM). This is called their **lowest common denominator**. Change to an equivalent fraction then add or subtract:

$$\frac{3}{8} + \frac{1}{2} = \frac{3}{8} + \frac{4}{8} = \frac{7}{8}$$

$$\frac{3}{5} - \frac{1}{2} = \frac{6}{10} - \frac{5}{10} = \frac{1}{10}$$

Multiplying fractions and integers

Multiplying a fraction by a whole number (integer) is the same as adding together that number of the fraction.

$3 \times \frac{1}{4}$ is the same as $\frac{1}{4} + \frac{1}{4} + \frac{1}{4} = \frac{3}{4}$

This can be written as $3 \times \frac{1}{4} = \frac{3}{4}$ ← The numerator is multiplied by the integer.

$5 \times \frac{1}{2} = \frac{5}{2} = 2\frac{1}{2}$ ← Change the **improper fraction** to a **mixed number**.

$8 \times \frac{3}{16} = \frac{24}{16} = 1\frac{8}{16} = 1\frac{1}{2}$

Keywords	lowest common denominator
	improper fraction mixed number

Answers

Ordering numbers

1 a $5 < 6$ b $3 > 2$ c $75 > 53$
  d $11 < 22$ e $1.75 < 5.32$

2 a $-7, -6, -1, 2, 5, 8$
  b $-17, -12, -11, 4, 11, 12$
  c $-9, -7, -5, 4, 6, 8$
  d $-5, -4, -3, 3, 6, 9$
  e $-8, -3, -2, 1, 4, 8$

Adding and subtracting positive and negative numbers

1 a -9 b -17 c 0 d 9 e 25

Using positive and negative numbers

1 a i 11°C   ii 23°C
  b i 0°C   ii 12°C
  c i -17°C   ii -5°C
  d i -11°C   ii 1°C
  e i -5°C   ii 7°C

2

-5	$+2$	-6
-4	-3	-2
0	-8	-1

Equivalent values

1 a $\frac{43}{100}$ b $\frac{57}{100}$

  c $\frac{24}{100} = \frac{6}{25}$ d $2\frac{65}{100} = 2\frac{13}{20}$

2 a 0.75   b 0.4
  c 0.625   d 4.33333…

3 a Fraction: $\frac{25}{100} = \frac{1}{4}$ Decimal: 0.25

  b Fraction: $\frac{40}{100} = \frac{2}{5}$ Decimal: 0.4

  c Fraction: $\frac{5}{100} = \frac{1}{20}$ Decimal: 0.05

  d Fraction: $\frac{88}{100} = \frac{22}{25}$ Decimal: 0.88

4 a 60%   b 16%   c 85%   d 86%
  e 67%   f 59%   g 12.5% h 37.5%

5 a $=$ b $>$ c $<$
  d $=$ e $=$ f $=$

Ratio and proportion

1 a 2:3   b 1:4
  c 1:3:4   d 4:5:10

2 a £54, £90   b 225g, 525g
  c 210ml, 270ml   d 1200km, 1500km

Direct proportion

1 a £2.40   b £3.60   2 $152

3 a 500g flour, 256g sugar, 256g margarine
     and 900g apples
  b 375g flour, 192g sugar, 192g margarine
     and 675g apples

Multiples

1 4, 8, 12, 16, 20   2 5, 10, 15, 20, 25
3 7, 14, 21, 28, 35   4 10, 20, 30, 40, 50
5 12, 24, 36, 48, 60   6 20, 40, 60, 80, 100

Factors

1 a 1, 3, 5, 15   b 1, 2, 4, 8, 16
  c 1, 2, 4, 5, 10, 20
  d 1, 2, 3, 4, 6, 8, 12, 24
  e 1, 2, 3, 5, 6, 10, 15, 30
  f 1, 3, 5, 9, 15, 45

2 a LCM: 60 HCF: 4   b LCM: 56 HCF: 2
  c LCM: 70 HCF: 5   d LCM: 90 HCF: 3
  e LCM: 90 HCF: 15   f LCM: 36 HCF: 9

Primes

1 23, 29   2 37, 41   3 71, 73, 79   4 97

Letters in algebra

1 a $c + 11$ b $10 - c$ c $6 - c$ d $4c + 3$
  e $2c - 5$ f $\frac{15}{c}$ g $2(c + 3)$

2 a $a + 2$ b $b - 4$ c $2n + 3c$ d $m - 5d$

Working with letters

1 a $8p$ b $7q + 5r$ c $4s - 2t$ d $5x - 3y$

2 a $12a$ b $2m - 5n + mn$

  c $\frac{2}{c}$ d $\frac{(ab + bc)}{cd}$

3 a $a = 4$ b $b = 20$ c $c = 11$ d $d = 5$

Forming an expression

1 a $m + 5$ b $2(2m + 5)$
2 i $5d + 12c$ ii $30t$ iii $4(3t + 5c)$
  b 111
3 $12r + 8w$

Simplifying expressions

1 a $2a + 2b + 1$ b $6c + 22$
  c $4d^2 - 7d$ d $4f + 6$

Substituting in expressions

1 a 6   b 11
  c 4   d 100

PAGE 17

Number sequences

1 26, 28, 30   2 66, 69, 72
3 64, 81, 100   4 125, 216, 343

Using shape patterns

1

2

Generating terms of a sequence

1 17, 20   2 84, 80
3 62.5, 31.25   4 405, 1215

PAGE 19

Further generating terms of a sequence

1 a 18   b 100   c 61   d 1600   e 39
2 a 196 b 26   c 51   d 100   e 248

Finding the nth term

1 a $3n - 2$ b $4n - 2$ c $4n - 1$ d $28 - 2n$
  e $2n + 1$ f $3n + 1$ g $n^2 + 1$ h $3 - n$

PAGE 21

Forming equations

1 $8n + 3 = 59$ $8n = 56$ $n = 7$
2 $t + t + 15 + t + 30 = 180$
   $3t + 45 = 180$ $3t = 135$ $t = 45$
   The three angles are 45°, 60° and 75°.
3 a $k + 5$ b $2(k + 5)$ or $2k + 10$
  c $2(k + 5) = 42$ $2k + 10 = 42$ $2k = 32$
     $k = 16$ marbles

Solving equations

1 $a = 20$ 2 $b = 4$ 3 $b = 12$ 4 $c = 21$
5 $c = 50$ 6 $d = 11$ 7 $d = 8$ 8 $e = 35$

PAGE 23

Solving more equations

1 a $f = 0$ b $f = 4$
2 a $a = 11$ b $b = 11$
3 a $g = 7$ b $g = 7$
4 a $a = 9$ b $b = 2$

Trial and improvement

1 $x = 1.4$ (1 decimal place)
2 $x = 5.4$ (1 decimal place)

PAGE 25

Using a formula

1 a $15cm^2$ b $15cm^2$
2 a 8cm   b 8cm
3 a 36cm   b 26cm
4 a 24cm   b 25mm

Substituting in a formula

1 a $y = 7$ b $c = 8$
2 a $A = 18$ b $r = 5$
3 a $s = 50$ b $D = 45$

Deriving a formula

1 $C = 27m$ 2 $c = 100n$
3 $C = £10 - 0.3y$ 4 $p = 100L$

PAGE 27

Functions and mappings

1 a
Input (x)	1	2	3	4	5	6
Output (y)	16	20	24	28	32	36

  b $y = 4(x + 3)$ or $f(x) = 4(x + 3)$
2 $f(x) = 3x$

Coordinates

1 a
x	-2	-1	0	1	2
y	-3	-2	-1	0	1

b
x	-2	-1	0	1	2
y	0	1	2	3	4

c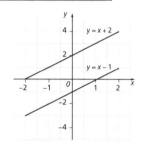

2 a Rectangle   b Isosceles triangle
  c Square

PAGE 29

Operations of number

1 a 392.632 b 785.156 c 608.255 d 117.387
2 a 4267   b 138
3 a 316.8cm   b 483 packets   c 54p

Order of operations

1 5   2 45   3 65   4 252

PAGE 31

Fractions of quantities

1 a 20p   b 400mm   c 750m   d 70cm
2 a $\frac{67}{100}$ b $\frac{55}{100} = \frac{11}{20}$ 3 a $\frac{33}{100}$ b $\frac{48}{100} = \frac{12}{25}$

Adding and subtracting fractions

1 a $\frac{3}{5}$ b $\frac{9}{11}$ c $\frac{19}{9} = 2\frac{1}{9}$
  d $\frac{9}{8} = 1\frac{1}{8}$ e $\frac{31}{30} = 1\frac{1}{30}$ f $\frac{17}{20}$
2 a $\frac{2}{15}$ b $\frac{7}{27}$ c $\frac{13}{20}$
  d $\frac{2}{12} = \frac{1}{6}$ e $\frac{3}{12} = \frac{1}{4}$ f $\frac{17}{20}$

Multiplying fractions and integers

1 $\frac{2}{7}$ 2 $\frac{15}{8} = 1\frac{7}{8}$ 3 $\frac{16}{9} = 1\frac{7}{9}$ 4 $\frac{4}{8} = \frac{1}{2}$

PAGE 33

Percentages of a quantity

1 a £8, £24   b £14, £56   c £3.50, £10.50
  d £30, £3   e £9, £4.50   f £56, £112
  g £72, £864   h £11, £33
2 a 360mm   b £9   c 45 mins   d 60

Calculating percentage change
1 a £15.40   b £180
2 a £23.75   b £56.32
3 £314.50   4 21°C

PAGE 35
Angles
1 a

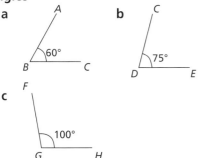

c

2 **a–c** Check the accuracy of measurement and estimate.
3 a 60°   b 45°   c 90°
4 a Reflex angle   b Acute angle
   c Right angle   d Obtuse angle
Angles on lines
a 85°   b 55°   c 52°   d 128°   e 128°

PAGE 37
Types of triangle
1–2

3 $\angle C = 60°$
4 $AC = 5cm$; $BC = 5cm$
5 Equilateral triangle (three equal sides, three equal angles)

Calculating the angles in a triangle
1 a 34°   b 68°
2 a 36°   c 35°   e 58°   g 15°
   b 72°   d 35°   f 58°   h 150°

PAGE 39
Types of quadrilateral

1

Quadrilateral	Sides and angles
Rectangle	Two pairs of equal sides; opposite sides parallel; four equal angles of 90°
Parallelogram	**Two pairs of equal sides; opposite sides parallel; opposite angles equal**
Rhombus	Four equal sides; opposite sides parallel; opposite angles equal
Trapezium	**One pair of parallel sides**
Isosceles trapezium	One pair of parallel sides; one pair of equal sides; two pairs of equal angles

2 **a–c** Check the accuracy of measurement of lines and angles, and that points marked *C* and *D* are joined.
   d $\angle C = 90°$, $\angle D = 90°$, $CD = 6cm$
   e Rectangle (two pairs of equal, parallel sides, four angles of 90°)
Calculating angles in a quadrilateral
1 101°   2 $\angle C = 85°$, $\angle E = 85°$, $\angle F = 95°$ 3 40°

PAGE 41
Parts of a circle

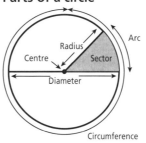

Circle formulae
1 a 12.56mm   b 21.98cm
2 a 200.96mm²   b 4.52cm² (2 d.p.)

PAGE 43
Parts of 3D shapes
1 a Cuboid   b 6 faces   c 12 edges
2 a 7 faces   b 15 edges   c 10 vertices
3 a   b   c

Nets of solids

PAGE 45
Moving shapes
1 a   b   c

d   e   f

2

Shape	A	B	C	D	E	F
Horizontal units	2	–4	4	9	8	–12
Vertical units	–2	–2	4	–4	4	0

Rotational symmetry
H and S (both order 2).

PAGE 47

Coordinates in four quadrants
1 A (–5, 1), B (–4, 6), C (–3, –3), D (–1, 0),
E (0, –2), F (0, 4), G (1, 4), H (2, 0), I (6, 2),
J (2, –2), K (5, –4)
2 Triangle   3 Trapezium
4 Quadrilateral   5 Right-angled triangle

Shapes and coordinates
1 (5, 5)   2 Any point with $x = 1$ and $y < 1$
3 (1, 4)
4 Square or trapezium

PAGE 49

Units of measure
1 a 22mm b 3.3m 2 a 8500g b 4.26kg
3 a 5.53l b 2980ml 4 32 5 60 6 8

Imperial measures
1 a 3.7m   b 12 pints   c 13km   d 5kg
2 a 49.5l   b £59.85

PAGE 51

Area of right-angled triangles
204mm^2

Composite shapes
1 a

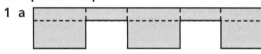

b 10.5cm^2
2 a 11m^2 b 600cm^2

Area of shapes made from parallelograms
1 a 5.04cm^2
  b 0.4cm^2
  c 4.64cm^2

PAGE 53

Probability scale
These answers should be correctly marked on
the probability scale.
1 $\frac{1}{6}$ 2 $\frac{5}{6}$ 3 $\frac{1}{2}$ 4 0   5 $\frac{4}{6} = \frac{2}{3}$

Equally likely outcomes
1 a $\frac{2}{11}$ b $\frac{4}{11}$ c $\frac{7}{11}$
2 a $\frac{2}{4} = \frac{1}{2}$ b $\frac{1}{4}$ c $\frac{1}{4}$
  d $\frac{2}{4} = \frac{1}{2}$ e 0   f 1

PAGE 55

Frequency charts

1

Mark	Tally	Frequency
11–20	I	1
21–30	III	3
31–40	IIII	5
41–50	IIII II	7
51–60	IIII	5
61–70	IIII I	6
71–80	III	3
	Total	30

2

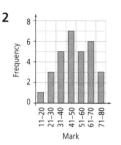

3 80
4 18

Scatter graphs
1 a Positive   b Negative
  c Positive   d Negative
2 Answers will vary. Possible answers include:
  a Distance travelled and petrol remaining
  b Shoe size and length of hair
  c Rainfall and sales of umbrellas

PAGE 57

Mode
1 2   2 10cm   3 £3.50

Median
1 6   2 2cm   3 1.75l

Mean
1 a 3.42   b 4.36g   c 11.5cm
2 a 4cm   b 0.15

PAGE 59

Interpreting pie charts
1 a Plum   b 25%
  c Plum, apple, cherry, pear, blackberry
2 a Interlocking plastic bricks
  b $\frac{1}{6}$ c 2   d 50%
e Wooden bricks

Comparing pie charts
1 30%   2 $\frac{2}{8} = \frac{1}{4}$ 3 £5   4 False   5 Tim

Fractions of quantities

1 Find the following quantities.

a $\frac{1}{5}$ of £1 _____

b $\frac{2}{3}$ of 600mm _____

c $\frac{3}{4}$ of 1km _____

d $\frac{7}{10}$ of 1 metre _____

2 Write the following as a fraction of £1.

a 67p _____

b 55p _____

3 Write the following as a fraction of 1 metre.

a 33cm _____

b 480mm _____

8

Adding and subtracting fractions

1 Add these fractions.

a $\frac{1}{5} + \frac{2}{5}$ _____

b $\frac{3}{11} + \frac{6}{11}$ _____

c $\frac{8}{9} + \frac{4}{9} + \frac{7}{9}$ _____

d $\frac{3}{8} + \frac{3}{4}$ _____

e $\frac{3}{10} + \frac{11}{15}$ _____

f $\frac{1}{4} + \frac{3}{5}$ _____

2 Subtract these fractions.

a $\frac{14}{15} - \frac{12}{15}$ _____

b $\frac{23}{27} - \frac{16}{27}$ _____

c $\frac{17}{20} - \frac{1}{5}$ _____

d $\frac{11}{12} - \frac{3}{4}$ _____

e $\frac{5}{6} - \frac{7}{12}$ _____

f $\frac{9}{10} - \frac{1}{20}$ _____

12

Multiplying fractions and integers

Multiply these fractions and integers.

1 $\frac{1}{7} \times 2$ _____

2 $\frac{3}{8} \times 5$ _____

3 $8 \times \frac{2}{9}$ _____

4 $4 \times \frac{1}{8}$ _____

4

TOTAL MARKS 24

Percentages of quantities

Percentages of a quantity

What is 20% of £320?

There are several methods you could use to solve this type of percentage question.

Method 1

Change to a fraction and work it out:

$20\% = \frac{20}{100} = \frac{1}{5}$

$\frac{1}{5}$ of £320 = £320 ÷ 5

$\qquad\qquad$ = £64

Method 2

Use 10% to work it out – just divide the number by 10:

10% of £320 is £32. So, 20% of £32 is double that: £64

Method 3

If you are allowed, use a calculator to work it out:

Key in:

20 ÷ 100 × 320 = ☐

Calculating percentage change

Percentage decrease

Discounts and sales often have percentage decreases.

A car costing £5600 has a 10% discount. What is the sale price?

To find 5%, remember that it is half of 10%.

Top tip!

Step 1

Work out the percentage:

10% of £5600 is £560.

Step 2

Take away this amount from the price:

£5600 − £560 = £5040

So the sale price of the car is £5040.

Percentage increase

For a percentage increase you add the percentage to the original amount.

A bottle normally has 920ml of olive oil, but this is increased by 5%. How much olive oil is now in the bottle?

Step 1

Work out the percentage:

5% of 920ml is 46ml.

Step 2

Add this to the original amount:

920 + 46 = 966

So the new amount is 966ml.

Percentages of a quantity

1 Write the percentages of each of these amounts.

a   £80

10% = £ [ ]

30% = £ [ ]

b   £140

10% = £ [ ]

40% = £ [ ]

c   £35

10% = £ [ ]

30% = £ [ ]

d   £300

10% = £ [ ]

1% = £ [ ]

e   £90

10% = £ [ ]

5% = £ [ ]

f   £5600

1% = £ [ ]

2% = £ [ ]

g   £7200

1% = £ [ ]

12% = £ [ ]

h   £220

5% = £ [ ]

15% = £ [ ]

2 Work out the following:

a   45% of 800mm _____

b   60% of £15 _____

c   75% of 1 hour _____

d   6% of 1000 _____

[12]

Calculating percentage change

1 Increase:

a   £14 by 10% _____

b   £150 by 20% _____

2 Decrease:

a   £25 by 5% _____

b   £64 by 12% _____

3 The price of a new washing machine is £370. This is discounted by 15% in a sale. What is the sale price?

_____

_____

4 The temperature of a pan of water is 20°C. It increases by 5% when heated. What is the new temperature?

_____

[6]

TOTAL MARKS [18]   33

PRACTISE   NUMBER AND ALGEBRA

Angles and lines

Angles

An angle is formed when two **line segments** meet at a point. The angle is the amount of turning (rotation) from one line to the other. It is measured, in degrees (°), using a protractor.

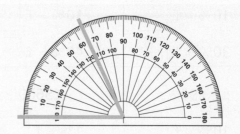

Place the base line of the protractor over the bottom line of the angle. The cross on the protractor is placed on the point of the angle. Use the scale that has 0° on the angle line.

This angle is 65° not 115°. Make sure you read the correct scale.

The angle opposite is described as $\angle B$, $\angle ABC$ or $A\hat{B}C$. It is at B, where AB and BC meet. B is called the **vertex**.

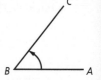

If the angle formed is 90°, the lines are **perpendicular**. A 90° angle is called a **right angle**.

An angle between 0° and 90° is an **acute angle**.

An angle between 90° and 180° is an **obtuse angle**.

An angle between 180° and 360° is a **reflex angle**.

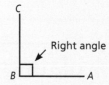

Angles on lines

All angles on a straight line add up to 180° ($a + b + c = 180°$).

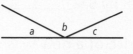

All angles at a point add up to 360° ($a + b + c + d = 360°$).

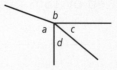

When two lines intersect (cross each other), they form two pairs of equal angles.

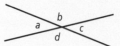

These are called vertically opposite angles ($a = c$ and $b = d$).

Top tip!

Keywords	line segment vertex perpendicular right angle
	acute angle obtuse angle reflex angle

Angles

1 Draw these angles on a separate piece of paper and label them.

    a ∠ABC 60°

    b ∠CDE 75°

    c ∠FGH 100°

2 Estimate these angles.

    a   **b**    **c**

    _____   _____   _____

3 Measure the angles in question **2** and compare them with your estimates.

    a _____   **b** _____   **c** _____

4 Which type of angles are these?

    a   **b** 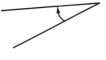   **c**   **d**

    _____   _____   _____   _____

13

Angles on lines

Calculate the angles marked with letters. Do not use a protractor.

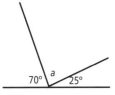   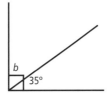   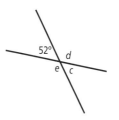

a _____   **b** _____   **c** _____

d _____   **e** _____

5

TOTAL MARKS   18

Triangles

Types of triangle

A **triangle** has three straight sides and three interior angles adding up to 180°. A triangle is a three-sided **polygon**.

Triangle	Sides and angles
	Triangle *ABC* has three different sides and three different angles. It is called a **scalene triangle**.
	A right-angled triangle has an angle of 90°. The side opposite the right angle is called the hypotenuse.
	An **equilateral triangle** has three equal sides and three equal angles.

Triangle	Sides and angles
	An **isosceles triangle** has two equal sides and two equal angles (opposite equal sides).
	An acute-angled triangle has three acute angles.
	An obtuse-angled triangle has one obtuse angle.

Calculating the angles in a triangle

The sum of the interior angles in a triangle is 180°. This means that if two angles are given, the third angle can be calculated.

A triangle *ABC* has $\angle A = 64°$ and $\angle B = 78°$. Calculate the third angle, $\angle C$.

Sum of angles in a triangle = 180°

$\angle C = 180° - (64° + 78°)$

$\angle C = 180° - 142° = 38°$

CDE is an isosceles triangle. $\angle C = \angle D$ and $\angle E = 72°$. Calculate $\angle C$ and $\angle D$.

$\angle C + \angle D + \angle E = 180°$

$\angle C = \angle D$

$\angle C + \angle D = 180° - 72° = 108°$

$\angle C = \angle D = \dfrac{108°}{2} = 54°$

FGH is an equilateral triangle. Calculate $\angle F$.

Sum of angles in a triangle = 180°

An equilateral triangle has three equal angles.

$\angle F = \dfrac{180°}{3} = 60°$ ← All three angles in an equilateral triangle = 60°

Keywords	triangle polygon scalene triangle equilateral triangle isosceles triangle

Types of triangle

1 Follow these instructions to draw a triangle.

- Draw a line, *AB*, 5cm in length.

- At *A* measure an angle of 60°.

- At *B* measure an angle of 60°.

2 Mark the point where these lines intersect *C*.

3 Measure ∠*C*. _____ cm

4 Measure *AC* and *BC*. _____ cm

5 Which type of triangle have you drawn? Explain your answer.

_____

7

Calculating the angles in a triangle

1 Calculate the third angle in these triangles.

a Triangle *ABC* has ∠*A* = 47° and ∠*B* = 99°.

Calculate ∠*C*. _____

b Triangle *DEF* has ∠*D* = 53° and ∠*E* = 59°.

Calculate ∠*F*. _____

2 These are all isosceles triangles. Find the missing angles.

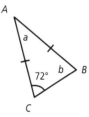 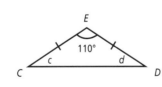 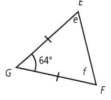 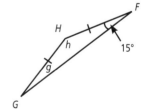

a _____   c _____   e _____   g _____

b _____   d _____   f _____   h _____

10

TOTAL MARKS 17   37

Quadrilaterals

Types of quadrilateral

A **quadrilateral** has four straight sides and four interior angles adding up to 360°. A quadrilateral is a four-sided polygon.

Quadrilateral	Sides and angles
Square	Four equal sides; opposite sides parallel; four equal angles of 90°
Rectangle	Two pairs of equal sides; opposite sides parallel; four equal angles of 90°
Parallelogram	Two pairs of equal sides; opposite sides parallel; opposite angles equal
Rhombus	Four equal sides; opposite sides parallel; opposite angles equal

Quadrilateral	Sides and angles
Trapezium	One pair of parallel sides
Isosceles trapezium	One pair of parallel sides; one pair of equal sides; two pairs of equal angles
Kite	Two pairs of adjacent equal sides; one pair of equal angles
Delta (arrowhead)	One pair of adjacent equal sides with included acute angle; one pair of adjacent equal sides with included obtuse angle

Calculating angles in a quadrilateral

The sum of the interior angles in a quadrilateral is 360°. This means that if three angles are given, the fourth angle can be calculated.

A quadrilateral $ABCD$ has $\angle A = 64°$, $\angle B = 78°$ and $\angle C = 105°$. Calculate $\angle D$.

Sum of angles in a quadrilateral = 360°

$\angle D = 360° - (64° + 78° + 105°)$

$\angle D = 360° - 247° = 113°$

$CDEF$ is a parallelogram.
$\angle C = \angle E = 72°$. Calculate $\angle D$ and $\angle F$.

$\angle C + \angle D + \angle E + \angle F = 360°$

$\angle D = \angle F$

$\angle D + \angle F = 360° - (2 \times 72°) = 216°$

$\angle D = \angle F = \dfrac{216°}{2} = 108°$

Keywords	quadrilateral

REVISE

GEOMETRY

Types of quadrilateral

1 Write the missing names and descriptions in the table.

Quadrilateral	Sides and angles
	Two pairs of equal sides; opposite sides parallel; four equal angles of 90°
Parallelogram	
	Four equal sides; opposite sides parallel; opposite angles equal
Trapezium	
	One pair of parallel sides; one pair of equal sides; two pairs of equal angles

2 Follow these instructions to draw a quadrilateral.

a Draw a line, *AB*, 6cm in length.

b At *A* measure an angle of 90° and a length of 4cm. Mark this point *D*.

c At *B* measure an angle of 90° and a length of 4cm. Mark this point *C*. Join *CD*.

d Measure ∠*C*, ∠*D* and *CD*.

_____

e Which type of quadrilateral have you drawn? Explain your answer.

_____

11

Calculating angles in a quadrilateral

Calculate the missing angle in these quadrilaterals.

1 Quadrilateral *ABCD* has ∠*A* = 74°, ∠*B* = 86° and ∠*C* = 99°. Calculate ∠*D*.   _____

2 Parallelogram *CDEF* has ∠*D* = 95°. Calculate ∠*C*, ∠*E* and ∠*F*.

_____   _____   _____

3 Kite *PQRS* has ∠*P* = 80° and ∠*Q* = ∠*S* = 120°. Calculate ∠*R*.   _____

5

TOTAL MARKS 16   39

Circles

Parts of a circle

A **circle** is a 2D curved shape. Its perimeter is called the **circumference** (*C*).

Each point on the circumference is the same distance from the centre of the circle. This is called the **radius** (*r*).

The distance across the circle, through the centre, is called the **diameter** (*d*) and is twice the length of the radius.

A **sector** is the area between two radii (plural of radius).

An **arc** is part of the circumference.

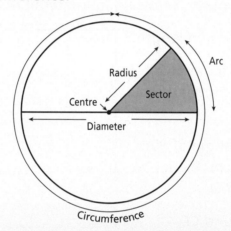

Circle formulae

If you divide the circumference of any circle by its diameter, the answer is always approximately 3. This is given by the Greek letter π (pi).

$\pi = \frac{C}{d} \approx 3.14 \approx \frac{22}{7}$ (or use the π key on a calculator)

Circumference of a circle (*C*) = π*d* or 2π*r*

Area of a circle (*A*) = πr^2

Remember to convert the diameter to radius.

Find the circumference and area of a circle which has a diameter of 5cm, using π = 3.14

$C = \pi d = 3.14 \times 5 = 15.7\text{cm}$

$A = \pi r^2 = 3.14 \times (2.5)^2 = 19.625 = 19.63\text{cm}^2$ (2 decimal places)

Keywords	circle circumference radius diameter sector arc

Parts of a circle

Label the parts of this circle.

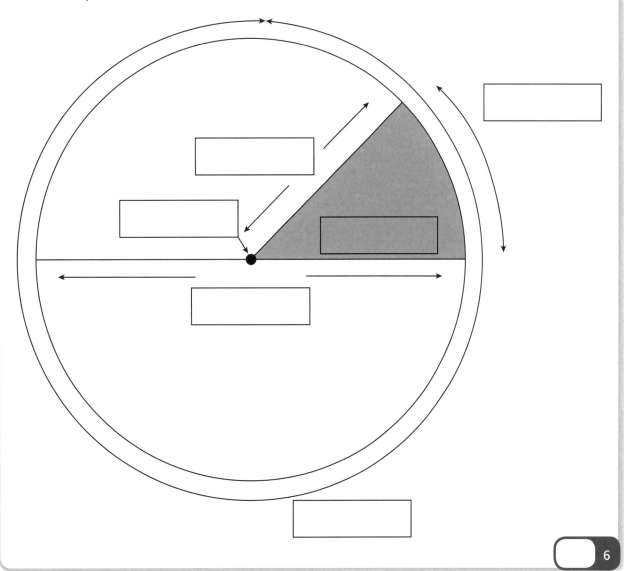

6

Circle formulae

❶ Find the circumference of these circles. Use π = 3.14

   a   Diameter = 4mm _____

   b   Radius = 3.5cm _____

❷ Find the area of these circles. Use π = 3.14

   a   Diameter = 16mm _____

   b   Radius = 1.2cm _____

4

3D shapes

Parts of 3D shapes

3D shapes are made up of **faces**, **edges** and vertices (plural of vertex).

A face is a surface of a solid.

An edge is where two faces meet.

A vertex (a corner) is where three or more edges meet.

A **cube** has 6 faces, 12 edges and 8 vertices.

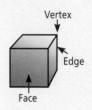

There is a relationship between the number of faces, edges and vertices of shapes. The Swiss mathematician, Euler, wrote it as a formula:
Number of faces + Number of vertices – Number of edges = 2
Test the formula F + V – N = 2 on different 3D shapes.

A **prism** is a 3D shape that has a constant cross-section.

3D shape		Faces	Edges	Vertices
Cuboid		6	12	8
Triangular prism		5 (2 △, 3 ▭)	9	6
Triangular-based pyramid (tetrahedron)		4	6	4

Nets of solids

The **net** of a shape is what it looks like when it is opened out flat.

Net of a cuboid

Net of a triangular prism

Keywords	face edge cube prism cuboid tetrahedron net

Parts of 3D shapes

1 There are two identical cubes.

    a If they are put together, what shape do they make? _____

    b How many faces does the new shape have? _____

    c How many edges does the new shape have? _____

2 A corner is cut off a cube.

    a How many faces does the new shape have? _____

    b How many edges does the new shape have? _____

    c How many vertices does the new shape have? _____

3 Draw prisms with the following cross-sections:

    a Right-angled triangle   **b** Pentagon

    c Isosceles trapezium

9

Nets of solids

Look at this net of a cube.

When it is folded up, which edge will meet the edge marked E? Mark it with an arrow.

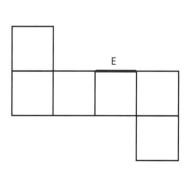

1

TOTAL MARKS 10

Transformations

Moving shapes

A shape can be moved by each of the following:

Rotation: a shape can be rotated about a point, **clockwise** or **anti-clockwise**.

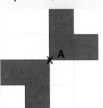

Shape A is rotated 180° around point X.

Reflection: this is sometimes called flipping over.

Shape A is reflected. The dotted line is a line of reflection.

Translation: this moves a shape a given distance horizontally and vertically. The image is the same size, but slides left (−) or right (+) and up (+) or down (−).

A translation is described by the distance and direction the shape has moved parallel to the *x*-axis and parallel to the *y*-axis. A coordinate grid should be used for a translation and remember to put + or − to show direction.

Triangle *ABC* is translated +3 units horizontally and +2 units vertically.

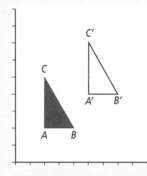

Rotational symmetry

If you can turn or rotate a shape and fit it onto itself in a different position to the original, then it has rotational **symmetry**. The red dots show the centre of rotation.

The order of rotational symmetry is the number of times the shape can turn to fit onto itself until it comes back to the original position.

This white cross has an order of rotational symmetry of 4:

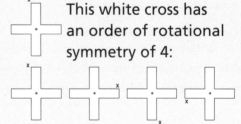

Keywords	rotation clockwise anti-clockwise reflection
	translation symmetry

Moving shapes

1 Copy the following shapes and reflect them in the dotted mirror line.

a 　b 　c 　d 　e 　f

2 In this diagram, A has been translated to A', B to B', and so on.

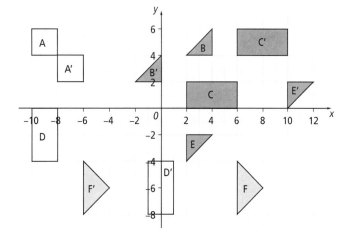

Give the units translated horizontally and vertically for each translated shape. The first one has been done for you.

Shape	A	B	C	D	E	F
Horizontal units	2					
Vertical units	−2					

11

Rotational symmetry

Circle the letters that have rotational symmetry.

M A T H S

For the letters you have circled, give the order of rotational symmetry.

_____

2

TOTAL MARKS　13

Coordinates

Coordinates in four quadrants

This coordinate grid is divided into four by the *x*-axis and the *y*-axis. Each part is called a **quadrant**.

Any point has the coordinates (*x*, *y*). *0* is the origin (0, 0).

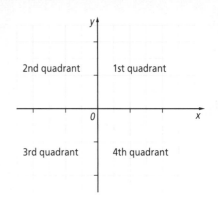

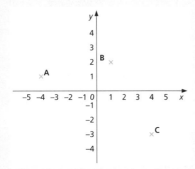

The coordinates of A are (–4, 1).

The coordinates of B are (1, 2).

The coordinates of C are (4, –3).

Coordinates are always written in brackets and separated by a comma. The numbers on the horizontal x-axis are written first, then the vertical y-axis. You can remember this because x comes before y and x is a cross!

Top tip!

Shapes and coordinates

Coordinates give the position of a point on a coordinate grid. Coordinates are useful in problems like the following:

The coordinates for two vertices of a rectangle are (–2, 1) and (2, 1). Give some possible coordinates of the two other vertices.

Two possible pairs of coordinates are:

(–2, –1) and (2, –1)

and

(–2, –2) and (2, –2)

There are many possible ways of forming a rectangle based on these two points. The two pairs of points shown each produce a rectangle.

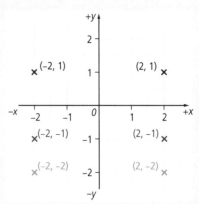

Keywords	quadrant

Coordinates in four quadrants

Points A–K are shown on this coordinate grid.

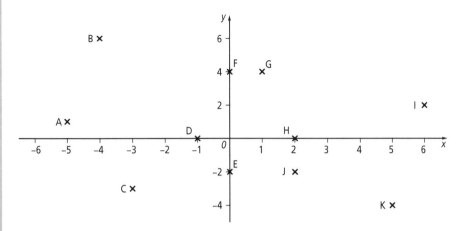

1 Write down the coordinates of each point.

A _____   B _____   C _____

D _____   E _____   F _____

G _____   H _____   I _____

J _____   K _____

2 Join the points ABDA to form a shape. What is it?   _____

3 Join the points ABDCA to form a shape. What is it?   _____

4 Join the points FGIHF to form a shape. What is it?   _____

5 Join the points EFJE to form a shape. What is it?   _____

15

Shapes and coordinates

Plot the points (–1, 3), (1, 5), (3, 3) on the axes alongside. What fourth point will make the following shapes?

1 Parallelogram   _____

2 Kite   _____

3 Arrowhead   _____

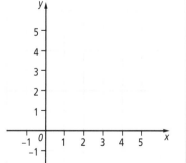

4 What other shapes can be made? _____

5

TOTAL MARKS 20

Measures

Units of measure

Length, weight (or mass) and capacity can be measured using **metric units**.

Length

1 centimetre (cm) = 10 millimetres (mm)

1 metre (m) = 100 centimetres (cm)

1 kilometre (km) = 1000 metres (m)

Weight

1 kilogram (kg) = 1000 grams (g)

1 tonne = 1000kg

Capacity

1 litre (l) = 1000 millilitres (ml)

1 centilitre (cl) = 10ml

It is important to write the units in your answers and remember that different units can be used for equivalent amounts.

This mirror is 1.825m or 1825mm high.

This bottle holds 2.855 litres or 2855 millilitres.

This feather weighs 0.064kg or 64g.

Imperial measures

We still sometimes use **imperial units**, which are measures that were used in the past. Try to learn these approximate metric values:

Length	**Weight**	**Capacity**
12 inches = 1 foot	16 ounces = 1 pound (lb)	8 pints = 1 gallon
2.5cm ≈ 1 inch	25g ≈ 1 ounce	1.75 pints ≈ 1 litre
30cm ≈ 1 foot	2.25lb ≈ 1kg	4.5 litres ≈ 1 gallon
3 feet ≈ 1 metre		
5 miles ≈ 8km		

Top tip!

Remember that ≈ means "is approximately equal to".

Keywords	metric units imperial units

Units of measure

1 Change these lengths to the unit in brackets.

   a   2.2cm (mm) _____   **b**   330cm (m) _____

2 Change these weights to the unit in brackets.

   a   8.5kg (g) _____   **b**   4260g (kg) _____

3 Change these capacities to the unit in brackets.

   a   5530ml (l) _____   **b**   2.98l (ml) _____

4 A jug holds 4 litres of fruit juice. How many 125ml cups will this fill?

_____

5 There is 50g of sauce in one bag. How many bags are there in a 3kg pack?

_____

6 During an athletics training session, Jenny runs 12 laps of a 400-metre track. She wants to run a total of 8km. How many more laps does she need to run?

_____

9

Imperial measures

1 Circle the best answer for each of these.

   a   A bus is 12 feet in height. Approximately how many metres is this?

      1.2m   2.5m   3.0m   3.7m   4.8m

   b   Approximately how many pints are there in 7 litres?

      7 pints   9 pints   12 pints   15 pints   18 pints

   c   Approximately how many kilometres are there in 8 miles?

      4km   7km   10km   13km   16km

   d   George catches an 11-pound fish. What is the approximate weight of the fish in kilograms?

      2kg   5kg   7kg   9kg   10kg

2 A petrol tank has a capacity of 11 gallons.

   a   How many litres does it hold? _____

   b   If petrol costs 120.9p per litre, how much does a tank of petrol cost?

_____

6

TOTAL MARKS   15

Area

Area of right-angled triangles

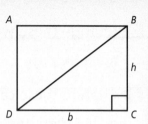

Here is a rectangle, *ABCD*. A diagonal line joins *B* and *D*, dividing the rectangle into two equal right-angled triangles.

Each triangle has a base *b* and height *h*.

b = length of rectangle (base of triangle *BCD*)

h = width of the rectangle (perpendicular height of triangle *BCD*)

Area of right-angled triangle $BCD = \frac{1}{2} \times$ Area of rectangle $ABCD = \frac{1}{2} \times b \times h$

The area of any triangle is given by the formula $A = \frac{1}{2}bh$ where *b* is the base of the triangle and *h* is the perpendicular height.

Composite shapes

A **composite shape** is made by combining two or more shapes. Find the area of each part and then add them together.

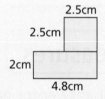

Area of rectangle is 4.8cm × 2cm = 9.6cm²
Area of square is 2.5cm × 2.5cm = 6.25cm²
Total area = 9.6cm² + 6.25cm² = 15.85cm²

Area of shapes made from parallelograms

A parallelogram is like a rectangle with two sloping sides. Its area is found by multiplying its base by its perpendicular height.

$A = b \times h = bh$

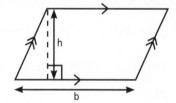

This wall tile is made from two parallelograms. Find the area of the tile.

Area of tile = 2(15 × 8)
= 2 × 120
= 240cm²

The perpendicular height must be used, not the side, i.e. 8cm not 10cm.

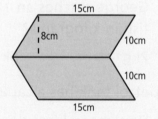

Keywords	composite shape

Area of right-angled triangles

What is the area of a right-angled triangle with base 24mm and height 17mm?

_____

Composite shapes

❶ This diagram shows the cross-section of a strip of wood.

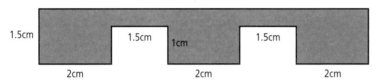

1.5cm   1.5cm 1cm   1.5cm

2cm   2cm   2cm

a   Draw dotted lines to show how to divide it into the least number of rectangles.

b   What is the area of the cross-section? _____

❷ What is the shaded area of flag **a** and frame **b**.

a

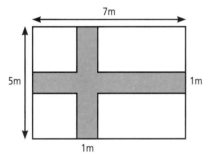

7m

5m   1m

1m

b

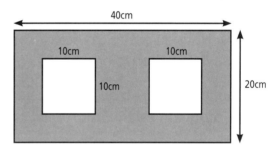

40cm

10cm   10cm

10cm   20cm

_____   _____

4

Area of shapes made from parallelograms

❶ This pattern is in the shape of a parallelogram with a small parallelogram cut out.

Find the area of...

a   the large parallelogram

   _____

b   the cut-out parallelogram

   _____

c   the shaded area

   _____

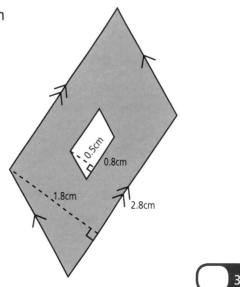

0.5cm
0.8cm
1.8cm
2.8cm

3

TOTAL MARKS   8   51

Probability

Probability scale

Probability (P) is the chance or risk that an event will happen. A probability scale can show how likely an event is to happen:

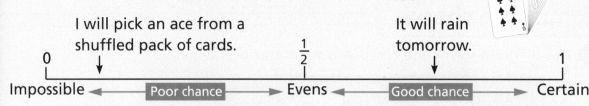

I will pick an ace from a shuffled pack of cards.

$\frac{1}{2}$

It will rain tomorrow.

0   1

Impossible ←   Poor chance   → Evens ←   Good chance   → Certain

0 is impossible – there needs to be absolutely no chance of it happening, and 1 is certain – it will absolutely, definitely happen. Most events lie somewhere in between these two extremes.

Top tip!

Equally likely outcomes

With activities involving 'chance', such as rolling dice, playing cards, coin tossing or spinners, you can use probability to decide on the possible or likely outcomes. Even chance is an equal chance of something happening as not happening. We also say a 1 in 2 chance or a 50:50 chance.

Tossing a coin has an even chance of landing on heads. It has two outcomes: heads or tails

$$P(head) = P(tail) = \frac{1}{2}$$

Rolling a dice has six outcomes: 1 or 2 or 3 or 4 or 5 or 6

$$P(1) = P(2) = P(3) = P(4) = P(5) = P(6) = \frac{1}{6}$$

It also has two outcomes: even number or odd number

$$P(\text{even number}) = P(\text{odd number}) = \frac{3}{6} = \frac{1}{2}$$

Look at this bag of beads. There are 12 beads and 6 of them are red.

What is the probability of picking out a red bead?

$\frac{6}{12}$ is the same as $\frac{1}{2}$, so there is a 1 in 2, or even, chance of picking out a red bead.

What is the probability of picking out one of the two blue beads in the bag?

$\frac{2}{12}$ is the same as $\frac{1}{6}$, so there is a 1 in 6 chance. In theory, this means that for every 6 beads picked out, 1 would be blue.

Keywords	probability event probability scale
	outcome even chance

Probability scale

A dice with numbers 1–6 is thrown. Write down the answers to these questions and mark them on the probability scale.

0 $\frac{1}{2}$ 1

1 What is the probability of getting a 6?   _____

2 What is the probability of **not** getting a 6?   _____

3 What is the probability of getting an even number?   _____

4 What is the probability of getting a zero?   _____

5 What is the probability of getting a number greater than 2? _____

5

Equally likely outcomes

1 Each letter of the word MATHEMATICS is written on a piece of card.
   The cards are put in a bag.

   What is the probability of picking each of the following?

   a A letter A   _____   b A vowel   _____

   c A consonant   _____

2 This spinner is divided into quarters.

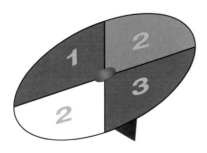

   What is the probability of getting each of the following?

   a A red quarter   _____   b A white quarter   _____

   c A number 1   _____   d An odd number   _____

   e A number 5   _____   f A number less than 4 _____

9

TOTAL MARKS   14   53

Handling data

Frequency charts

The word frequency means 'how many' or 'how often', so a frequency chart shows how many there are in a group or how often something happens.

A bar chart can represent discrete data or grouped data.

Each bar is equal in width. The height of the bar = frequency.

The bar chart above right shows the favourite type of television programmes of a group of people.

Frequency charts with grouped data are useful for comparing large groups of numbers.

An airport wanted to compare the weights of the luggage put onto a plane. It was better to group the data to compare them.

Top tip!

A frequency table can be used to record and group a collection of numbers before drawing a bar graph to show the information.

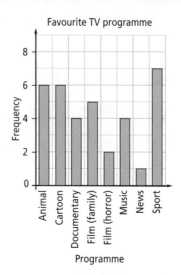

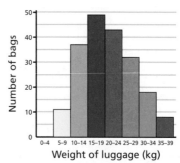

The most common weight of luggage is between 15kg and 19kg.

Scatter graphs

A scatter graph compares two sets of data plotted against each other. If there is a relationship between them it is called correlation.

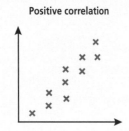
Positive correlation

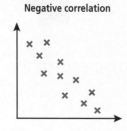
Negative correlation

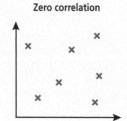
Zero correlation

Keywords	frequency bar chart discrete data
	scatter graph correlation

REVISE

STATISTICS

Frequency charts

The marks for an English exam are as follows:

53	52	67	70	45	30
35	45	63	55	75	79
44	38	50	58	39	60
64	29	80	18	70	35
65	37	43	49	29	41

1 On a separate piece of paper, group the marks and put the information into a frequency table.

2 On a separate piece of paper, draw a bar chart.

3 What is the highest mark? _____

4 What is the lowest mark? _____

4

Scatter graphs

1 Is the correlation between these sets of data **positive** or **negative**?

a Temperature and number of ice-creams sold _____

b The age of a car and its value _____

c The height and weight of a person _____

d Heat loss and insulation _____

2 Give an example of two sets of data giving each of the following:

a A negative correlation

_____

b A zero correlation

_____

c A positive correlation

_____

7

Averages

Mode

The mode of a set of data is the value that occurs most often.

These are the Maths test scores out of 20 for a group of children:

18   16   14   18   12   13   17   12   16   16   15   11

The modal average for these scores is 16.

Median

The median is the middle value in a set of data arranged in order starting with the smallest value. This is called ascending order.

 When working out the median for an even amount of numbers, you take the two middle numbers, add them together and divide by two.

This chart shows the number of letters received each day for a week.

Monday	Tuesday	Wednesday	Thursday	Friday	Saturday	Sunday
5 letters	4 letters	8 letters	5 letters	3 letters	4 letters	1 letter

To work out the median number of letters, follow these two steps:

1. Put the numbers in ascending order: 1, 3, 4, 4, 5, 5, 8.
2. Go to the middle number: 1, 3, 4, **4**, 5, 5, 8.   So the median is 4 letters.

Mean

The mean is what most people refer to as the average.

The mean of a set of numbers = $\dfrac{\text{Sum of the numbers in the set}}{\text{The number of items in the set}}$

This table shows the number of bikes sold from a shop over four weeks.

Week 1	Week 2	Week 3	Week 4
9	14	18	23

 The range tells us how much the information is spread. To find the range, work out the difference between the largest and smallest value.

Mean = $\dfrac{\text{Sum}}{\text{Number of items}}$

$9 + 14 + 18 + 23 = 64$ $\dfrac{64}{4} = 16$

So the mean average number of bikes sold in a week is 16.

Keywords   mode   median   mean   range

Mode

Work out the mode of the following sets of numbers.

1 0, 3, 2, 5, 5, 2, 3, 1, 2, 0, 2 _____

2 11cm, 13cm, 12cm, 13cm, 12cm, 10cm, 10cm, 11cm, 10cm _____

3 £3.50, £2.75, £4, £3.50, £2.50, £4, £2.50, £3.50 _____

[3]

Median

Work out the median of the following sets of numbers.

1 5, 7, 7, 4, 3, 6, 8

_____

2 3cm, 3cm, 1cm, 1.5cm, 2cm, 2cm, 2.5cm

_____

3 1.5l, 1.75l, 1.8l, 1.9l, 1.75l, 1.9l, 1.5l

_____

[3]

Mean

1 Calculate the mean of the following sets of numbers.

a 2.1, 3.2, 4.3, 1.5, 6

_____

b 4g, 2.5g, 5g, 3g, 7.3g

_____

c 12.3cm, 14cm, 10.5cm, 11.7cm, 9cm

_____

2 What is the range of the following sets of numbers?

a 125cm, 123cm, 122cm, 121cm, 124cm _____

b 0.25, 0.34, 0.27, 0.38, 0.26, 0.30, 0.23 _____

[5]

TOTAL MARKS [11]

Pie charts

Interpreting pie charts

Pie charts are circles divided into sectors. The sectors represent the proportions of each item of data in a set. The sector angles are fractions of a full circle (360°). You could be asked to give a fraction, a percentage or a number as an answer.

A class library has 60 books. This pie chart shows the three types of books.

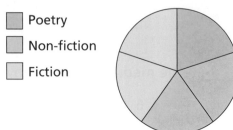

- Poetry
- Non-fiction
- Fiction

What fraction of the books are non-fiction?
Look at the total number of sectors and the fraction of them that are non-fiction.
$\frac{2}{5}$ of the books are non-fiction books.

What percentage of the books are poetry?
$\frac{1}{5}$ of the books are poetry books. Change this to a percentage:

$$\frac{1}{5} = \frac{20}{100} = 20\%$$

So 20% of the books are poetry books.

How many books are fiction?
There are 60 books altogether and the pie chart is divided into five sectors, so each individual sector represents 12 books. Two of the sectors are fiction, which means that 24 of the books are fiction books.

Comparing pie charts

When you compare two pie charts, look carefully at the totals for each and at the number of sectors.

These pie charts show the results for two hockey teams. Team A played 24 matches and Team B played 18 matches.

It looks like the two teams have won the same number of matches, but compare them carefully.

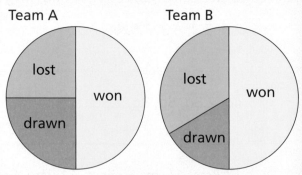

Team A   Team B

lost   won   drawn

lost   won   drawn

Team A have won $\frac{1}{2}$ of 24 matches, which is 12.

Team B have won $\frac{1}{2}$ of 18 matches, which is 9.

Top tip!

Always look at the total for the whole 'pie' and then work out what each sector is worth by seeing what fraction of the 'pie' it is.

Keywords	pie chart

Interpreting pie charts

1 This pie chart shows information on sales of fruit pies during October.

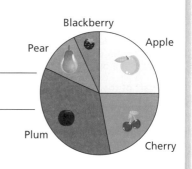

 a Which was the best selling pie for the month? _____

 b What percentage of sales were the apple pies? _____

 c List the pies sold in order of popularity.

_____

2 Six groups of children built toy towers from different materials. This pie chart shows the materials used by the six groups to build their towers.

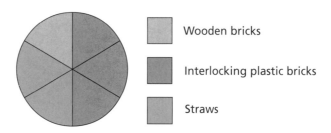

Wooden bricks

Interlocking plastic bricks

Straws

 a Which was the most popular choice of material to build a tower? _____

 b What fraction of the class used wooden bricks? _____

 c How many groups used straws? _____

 d What percentage of the class did **not** use plastic bricks? _____

 e Which type of material did only one group use? _____

8

Comparing pie charts

Tim and Ali bought some material from a DIY shop so they could each build a brick wall. These pie charts show the materials they each bought. Tim spent £250 and Ali spent £280.

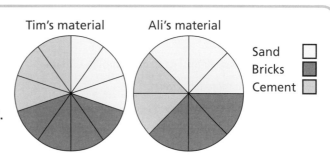

Tim's material   Ali's material

Sand
Bricks
Cement

1 What percentage of his money did Tim spend on sand? _____

2 What fraction of his money did Ali spend on cement? _____

3 How much more did Ali spend on bricks than Tim? _____

4 True or false? They both spent the same proportion of their total money on sand. _____

5 Who spent the most money on cement? _____

5

TOTAL MARKS 13

Glossary

GLOSSARY

acute angle an angle between 0° and 90°

anti-clockwise when something turns anti-clockwise, it rotates in the opposite direction to the hands of a clock

arc a part of the circumference of a circle

area the space covered by a 2D shape

axis (axes) x-axis: horizontal axis of a coordinate grid; y-axis: vertical axis of a coordinate grid

bar chart a chart that uses bars of equal width to represent data

BIDMAS **B**rackets; **I**ndices and roots; **D**ivision and **M**ultiplication; **A**ddition and **S**ubtraction; a useful way to remember the order of operations

circle a 2D shape with every point on its edge a fixed distance from its centre

circumference the edge or perimeter of a circle

clockwise when something turns clockwise, it rotates in the same direction as the hands of a clock

coefficient a number multiplying an algebraic term

composite shape a shape made from combining two or more shapes

coordinates (x, y) pairs of numbers giving the position of a point on a graph or grid

correlation the relationship between two variables

cube a 3D shape with six square faces

cuboid a solid shape with six rectangular faces

decimal a number based on 10

denominator the number below the line in a fraction

diameter the chord that passes through the centre of a circle

digit any of the 10 numerals from 0 to 9

direct proportion two quantities changing in the same ratio

discrete data separate or distinct items or groups of data

edge where two or more faces meet

equation a statement showing two equal expressions

equilateral triangle a triangle with all sides equal and all angles equal

equivalent two numbers or measures are equivalent if they are the same or equal

estimate an approximation of the actual value

even chance the same chance of something happening as not happening. The probability is $\frac{1}{2}$ or 0.5

event something that happens, e.g. tossing a coin

expression a mathematical statement having letters and numbers

face the flat surface, or side, of a solid shape

factor a whole number that divides exactly into a given number

formula an equation used to find quantities when given certain values

fraction part of the whole

frequency the number of times that something happens

function machine a diagram illustrating the sequence of operations in a procedure

highest common factor (HCF) the highest factor of two or more numbers

imperial units a system of weights and measurements used before the metric system was introduced (still used)

improper fraction a fraction which has a numerator greater than the denominator

isosceles triangle a triangle with two equal sides and two equal angles

line segment a part of a straight line

lowest common denominator the lowest common multiple of all the denominators in a set of fractions

lowest common multiple (LCM) the lowest number which is a multiple of two or more numbers

mapping changing something by following a given rule

mean an average value found by dividing the sum of a set of quantities by the number of quantities

median the middle item in an ascending sequence of items

metric units units in a number system based on multiples of 10

mixed number a whole number together with a proper fraction

mode an average value that is the most frequent value

multiple if a number divides exactly into another number, the second is a multiple of the first

negative number a number less than zero

net a surface which can be folded into a solid

nth term the general term of a number sequence

number line a line with a scale, showing numbers in order

numerator the number above the line in a fraction

obtuse angle an angle between 90° and 180°

order of operations the order in which arithmetic is carried out

origin the point where the x-axis and y-axis cross, with coordinates (0, 0)

outcome a possible result of an experiment or an event

percentage the proportion or rate per 100 parts

perimeter the boundary or length around the edge of an area

perpendicular a line at right angles or 90° to another line

pie chart a circular chart illustrating data

place value the value of a digit that relates to its place within a given number

polygon a 2D or plane shape made from straight lines

positive number a number greater than zero